Neath Abbey

David M. Robinson PhD, FSA

A History of the Abbey

A view of Neath Abbey from the north-west. The ruins represent two major buildings, a medieval Cistercian monastery and a large Tudor house. The remains of the great abbey church appear to the left of the view. The Tudor house, with its distinctive windows, can be seen in the centre, behind the ruins of the monastery's conventual buildings (ffotograff Picture Agency and Library).

'It semid to me the fairest abbay of al Wales' wrote the Tudor antiquary, John Leland (d. 1552), following his visit to Neath in the later 1530s. Ironically, his observations were made on the very eve of the Cistercian abbey's demise. In February 1539, after more than four centuries of unbroken observance, monastic life at Neath was brought to an abrupt end. The buildings and much of the former abbey estate were soon in the hands of an aspiring Tudor magnate. Thereafter, although the great abbey church was partially dismantled, the finer monastic apartments were pressed into new secular uses, with a fashionable gentry house erected over one corner of the complex. In due course, this too was abandoned and allowed to fall into decay. As a result, the ruins which survive at Neath today represent not one, but two major buildings: a medieval monastery and a large Tudor house. Together they span over 600 years of history.

Above: The ruins of the twelfth-century abbey at Savigny (Manche) in south-west Normandy. Founded by St Vitalis of Mortain (d. 1122), by the 1140s Savigny was the mother house of a flourishing monastic congregation with houses on both sides of the English Channel (David Robinson).

Right: The charter of 1130 in which Richard de Granville granted various properties to the abbey of the Holy Trinity at Savigny for the foundation of a daughter house at Neath (West Glamorgan Archive Service, A/N 1).

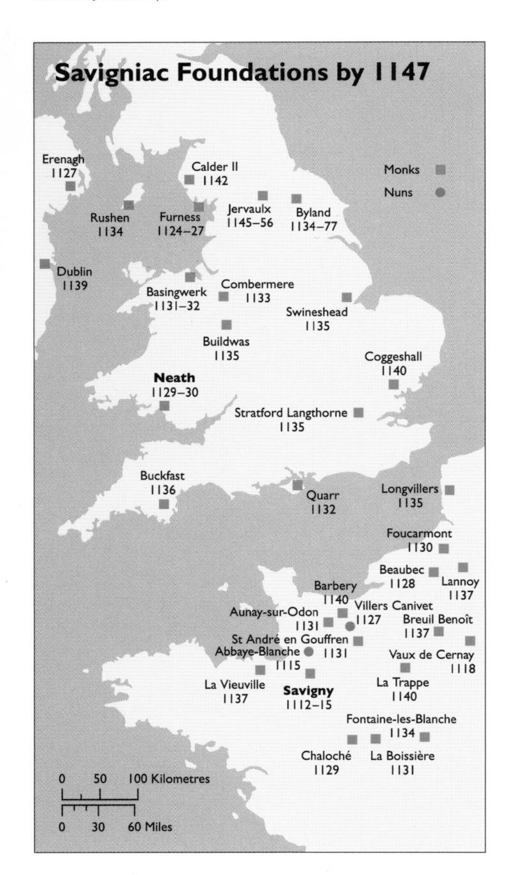

A Savigniac Foundation

The founder of Neath Abbey was Richard de Granville, military commander to the Anglo-Norman lord of Glamorgan, Earl Robert of Gloucester (d. 1147). As head of the earl's forces, Richard played a leading role in the further westward advance of Norman authority along the coastal lowlands of Glamorgan. Around 1120, in fact, he pushed into the Welsh territories beyond the river Neath, carving out a lordship and building a castle on the west bank to consolidate his gains.

By 1129, however, Richard had chosen to grant his estates at Neath to the Norman abbey of Savigny (Manche), an act of patronage in which he was joined by his wife, Constance. Towards the end of his charter of gifts — which included extensive lands between the Neath and Tawe rivers, together with meadows, mills, and the chapel of his castle — Richard made it clear that this property was intended to endow a new monastery. Happily, Savigny agreed to the arrangements, and soon sent out a daughter colony across the English Channel. Abbot Richard (d. 1145) and his twelve monks arrived at Neath in October 1130.

Richard de Granville may have chosen to support Savigny's particular brand of monasticism through personal knowledge of the house. Indeed, his family origins possibly lay at Granville, situated on the west coast of the Norman duchy not far

·om the abbey itself. But in any case, .ichard would doubtless have been in touch /ith the most fashionable ideas circulating mong other monastic patrons around ıis time. In other words, he was surely ware of the growing popularity of the avigniacs generally, and of the patronage estowed on them both by royalty, and y several important members of the nglo-Norman aristocracy.

The abbey of the Holy Trinity at Savigny ad itself been founded less than two ecades earlier by St Vitalis of Mortain 1. 1122). Around 1094, Vitalis had chosen abandon his career as a secular canon in vour of becoming a hermit and wandering reacher. In 1105, or thereabouts, he found s way to a forested area in south-west lormandy where he 'discovered the llage of Savigny ... and began to establish monastery'. Vitalis was joined at Savigny y a group of like-minded disciples, ncouraging him to compose a simple ıonastic code based on the *Rule of* : *Benedict* (see below). At some point etween 1112 and 1115, the fledgling ommunity saw its status raised to that f an abbey.

Under Abbot Geoffrey (1122–39), italis's experiment was transformed into flourishing monastic congregation. The avigniac family grew rapidly and soon omprised more than thirty monasteries, ith as many as half of these located ıroughout the British Isles. Yet, in spite f this success, there were always signs f weakness within the family. In particular, ıe Savigniac fathers had failed to establish ıy effective machinery for the governance f their various daughter houses.

As internal pressure for change creased, Abbot Serlo (1140–53) began fear for the future of the congregation. leanwhile, he had been greatly influenced y the success of the Cistercians, and articularly by the charisma of their chief ɔokesperson, St Bernard of Clairvaux 1. 1153). Finding the problems too urdensome to contend with alone, Serlo etitioned for his entire Savigniac family to e absorbed into the Cistercian order. The ıerger was approved by the Cistercians : their General Chapter meeting of 1147.

Cistercian Neath

Henceforth, the fledgling community at Neath — along with all other British and French Savigniac abbeys — was to become part of the most successful and highly regarded religious order in medieval Europe. Beginning with the foundation of the abbey at Cîteaux (Côte d'Or) in Burgundy in 1098, by the mid- to late 1140s the Cistercian family already comprised close to 300 directly affiliated abbeys. In due course, the total number was to rise to more than 700.

Almost from the first, the Cistercians were determined to distinguish themselves from other monks, and worked hard to forge a self-identity. Above all, they took as their supreme guide the *Rule of St Benedict*, which had been written shortly after AD535 by the father of western monasticism, St Benedict of Nursia. Following the *Rule*, they were committed to a radical simplification of monastic practice, turning away from all sources of excessive luxury and wealth. Their buildings were to be plain and devoid of sculpture, with a similar degree of austerity imposed on the appearance of liturgical books, vessels and ornaments. They chose an economy based upon the direct exploitation of land, initially worked by an army of lay brothers (*conversi*) who lived as

St Benedict of Nursia — the father of western monasticism. In this manuscript illumination of 1173, the saint holds a copy of his Rule, *written soon after AD 535. The Cistercians sought to follow Benedict's* Rule *to the letter, leading to their radical simplification of contemporary monastic practice (Stiftsbibliothek Zwettl, Ms. 10, f. 46r).*

One of the chief hallmarks of the early Cistercians was their direct exploitation of agricultural land, as depicted in this thirteenth-century manuscript illustration. They recruited large numbers of lay brothers, known as conversi *(converts), to undertake much of the manual labour (Cambridge University Library, Ms. Mm. 5.31, f. 113r).*

part of each abbey community. Instead of the traditional black robes of the Benedictines, the Cistercians wore habits of undyed wool, giving rise to their popular name, the white monks. They also rejected undershirts and breeches, followed a strict rule of silence, and at first survived on a meagre vegetarian diet.

The Twelfth and Thirteenth Centuries

The monks at Neath appear to have made the transition to the Cistercian way of life without too much difficulty. Their economy certainly came to be highly dependent upon the direct and intensive cultivation of agricultural land. At the heart of the community's estate was Richard de Granville's endowment of 'all the waste which lies between the waters of the Neath, Tawe, Clydach and Pwll Cynan', perhaps up to 10 square miles (26km^2) of country. Within sixty years, the monks had moved from this base to control an enviable group of properties across the lordships of Glamorgan and Gower, and as far afield as Devon and Somerset.

Despite its extent, however, the abbey's estate was far too dispersed to be managed efficiently. In point of fact, such was the precarious position in which the community found itself in the late 1190s, careful thought was given to moving the entire abbey to the site of its property at Exford in north-west Somerset. Any hope of realizing this plan was eventually abandoned following the foundation of Cleeve Abbey in 1197–98, barely 10 miles (16km) from Exford. Instead, the Neath monks began a concerted effort to consolidate their holdings nearer to home. In the face of a series of bitter land disputes fought with the neighbouring Cistercian house at Margam (continuing into the early thirteenth century), by the 1290s Neath had become one of the richest monasteries in Wales. Its annual income at that time was about £236, exceeded only by Margam's figure of £256.

Up to this point, wherever possible the abbey's lands had been organized into distinctive and compact farms, known as granges. Worked by a devout army of lay brothers, the grange was the key to the early success of Cistercian land management. Neath's grange at Monknash in the Vale of Glamorgan, for example, where excellent earthworks and some buildings survive, covered something in excess of 800 acres (324ha). In all, by the 1290s the Neath monks were recorded as farming an arable estate of more than 5,000 acres (2,024ha). Their livestock numbers included almost 5,000 sheep and around 220 cattle; they also held urban property in the boroughs of Caerleon, Cardiff, Cowbridge and Neath.

Growth of the Abbey Buildings

At first, the Savigniac monks who settled at Neath in the early 1130s may have been accommodated in temporary wooden structures, possibly at the founder's castle. But it cannot have been too long before

Any plan for Neath Abbey to relocate to its property at Exford in north-west Somerset was abandoned when, in 1197–98, Cleeve Abbey was founded barely 10 miles (16km) away (English Heritage).

The key to the success of early Cistercian land management was the grange, a compact farm worked by the lay brothers. Neath's grange at Monknash in the Vale of Glamorgan covered over 800 acres (324ha). Extensive earthworks and some ruined buildings, seen here from the air, mark the site of the grange's nucleus (Royal Commission on the Ancient and Historical Monuments of Wales).

tone buildings were begun on the permanent te. In particular, the construction of an bbey church, almost certainly in an austere omanesque style, must have been the nain priority, though some twelfth-century rogress with the monastic buildings is also be expected. Indeed, the west range — ow the earliest surviving upstanding tructure — is unlikely to have been started nuch later than the 1170s, and it may well ncorporate earlier masonry (p. 14).

It was probably the growing number of nonks and lay brothers within the abbey ommunity that led to the need for fresh uilding campaigns. In the event, substantial rogrammes of reconstruction were to un from the beginning of the thirteenth entury through to the mid-fourteenth entury. The work began with two of the rincipal ranges of monastic buildings, those n the east and south sides of the cloister. ere, the chapter house, the monks' day oom, the dormitory, the warming house, nd the monks' refectory were all almost ntirely rebuilt during the second quarter f the thirteenth century (pp. 12–13).

Having completed this phase, during ne abbacy of Adam of Carmarthen (about 266–89) the community decided it was me to replace its twelfth-century church ith a brand new building on a much rger scale (pp. 8–11). This second nurch was designed in the fast emerging ecorated architectural style, with the ork of construction running from about 280 through into the first decades of ne fourteenth century. In 1284, at an arly stage of the programme, the site as visited by King Edward I (1272–1307). o mark his visit, the king presented the ommunity with 'a very beautiful baldachin', ossibly a canopy intended for the high altar.

Left: It was probably the building of the new abbey church by Abbot Adam of Carmarthen (1266–89) that brought King Edward I (1272–1307) to Neath in 1284. Edward presented 'a very beautiful baldachin', possibly a canopy for the high altar, to the community to mark his visit. The coronation of the king is depicted in this near-contemporary manuscript illustration (Chetham's Library, Manchester, Ms. 6712 (A.6.89), f. 247v/Bridgeman Art Library).

Below: Although the detail is open to reinterpretation, this reconstruction drawing provides a general impression of the abbey's appearance in the mid-fourteenth century. The monastic buildings (in the right foreground) had been constructed in the twelfth and thirteenth centuries. The abbey church (to the rear left) was designed in the Decorated architectural style and was completed about 1330 (Illustration by Dylan Roberts, RCAHMW).

The Later Middle Ages

n 1289, it was probably the need to raise ard cash to finance the building of the ew church that prompted Abbot Adam o enter into an exchange agreement ith Gilbert de Clare, earl of Gloucester 1263–95). Under the terms of this greement, Adam handed over very large tracts of land to Earl Gilbert in return for £100 of fixed annual rents. It was an important milestone in the abbey's history, representing the first move away from the ideals of grange farming in favour of a rentier economy. The monks took another significant step in this direction in 1322, when the Somerset property of Exford was leased out for the first time.

Over the course of the fourteenth and early fifteenth centuries, the community was obliged to cope with an ongoing catalogue of difficulties, all contributing to a further abandonment of the idealistic grange economy. In 1316, for example, during the uprising in south Wales led by Llywelyn Bren, damage inflicted on the abbey's estates was said to have left the monks 'plundered of their goods ... their house devastated and ruined'. The situation can only have been exacerbated by the Black Death of 1348–50, and then by the effects of the Owain Glyn Dŵr rebellion in the early fifteenth century. As late as 1423, Neath was said to be suffering grievously from indiscriminate pillaging; the abbey had been violated, robbed of its books, chalices and ornaments.

On the long road to recovery, the first steps seem to have been taken by the very able Abbot Thomas Franklin (1424–41), a Cistercian reformer of considerable stature. He was eventually commended by the pope for his success in having repaired and restored Neath, increasing the number of monks, improving the quality of its worship, and the wealth of its possessions. Building on this, the community received further support from Richard Neville (d. 1471), earl of Warwick and lord of Glamorgan, who granted the house an important charter of confirmation in 1468.

By the turn of the fifteenth century, such was the fresh confidence of one of Neath's early Tudor abbots that he began to build himself a major new suite of private accommodation (p. 14). Situated at the far south-eastern corner of the claustral complex, the creation of these new lodgings involved a degree of conversion of several former communal chambers, including the monks' dormitory and latrine. These changes say much about the greatly reduced size of the abbey community in the later Middle Ages. Indeed, there were fewer than ten monks in residence by this time.

Nevertheless, conventual life at the house was to reach new heights under its last head, Leyshon Thomas (about 1510–39), undoubtedly one of Neath's greatest abbots. An Oxford graduate, and a man of considerable learning, he became an influential figure in the Cistercian order at large. So great was Leyshon's scholarly reputation, not to mention his bountiful hospitality, the poet Lewis Morgannwg was moved to lavish enormous praise on the unrivalled beauty of his monastery: 'Splendid is the court beside the sea', he wrote, 'warmth of hospitality graces this well-appointed retreat, and the meals befit the generous'. Lewis was also rapturous in his praise of the abbey buildings, concluding: 'No abode of the living, no roofed building or house of nobles; no such foundations or graceful erections, no oak beams of like length unto these was or ever will be'.

In 1535, just before King Henry VIII's suppression of the monasteries began, Neath's annual income was assessed at £132. The community somehow managed to escape the first round of monastery closures in the following year, and in January 1537 Abbot Leyshon paid a heavy fine of £150 to prolong the life of his house still further. Dearly bought, the reprieve lasted barely two years. In February 1539, the abbot and his seven remaining monks finally surrendered their house to the king's visitors.

In the 1590s the Neath Abbey estate was purchased by Sir John Herbert (d. 1617), who held high office under both Elizabeth I and James I. Sir John may well have introduced further improvements to the post-suppression house. His tomb effigy lies in St John's Church, Cardiff.

After the Suppression

Soon after its closure, the site of the abbey and the bulk of its former estates were leased to Sir Richard Williams alias Cromwell (d. 1545). Interestingly, he was a nephew of Thomas Cromwell (d. 1540), the architect behind the suppression of the monasteries. In March 1542, Sir Richard was allowed to buy the properties outright for £731. The immediate fate of the abbey buildings is unclear, though as late as 1547 there was apparently still some two tons of lead on the roofs of various buildings.

It was perhaps Sir Richard who began to adapt the late medieval abbot's residence as a new secular dwelling. However, its full transformation into a splendid Tudor great house has been dated on stylistic grounds to about 1560, and it is therefore more likely to have been the work of Sir Richard's son, Henry. In any case, in the 1590s, Francis Williams alias Cromwell sold the house and estate to Sir John Herbert (1550–1617). Sir John, who held high office under Elizabeth I (1558–1603) and James I (1603–25), and was MP for Glamorgan in 1601, may well have introduced further improvements to the building. When he died in 1617, the

state passed via his daughter, Mary, to Sir
William Dodington (d. 1638) of Hampshire.
heir son, Edward Dodington, in turn
ransferred it to his nephew, Sir Philip Hoby
d. 1678). Sir Philip's widow, Elizabeth, seems
o have remained at the abbey house until
er death in 1699, after which the estate
vas divided between three daughters. One
f these married Griffith Rice (d. 1729)
f Dynevor, whose descendants held the
roperty through into the twentieth century.

Meanwhile, during the first half of the
ighteenth century, industry began to
nvade the abbey site. In 1731, a manager
or the Welsh Copper Company took out
lease on the property and introduced
he processes associated with copper
melting and forging. Even so, if we are to
elieve the evidence of the engraving of
Neath produced by the brothers Samuel
nd Nathaniel Buck, in the early 1740s the
udor house apparently remained occupied
nd complete, its roofs intact and chimneys
moking. But, as the century progressed, it
vas definitely abandoned and allowed to
all into ruin, as shown, for instance, in a
ainting by J. M. W. Turner of about 1795.

Thereafter, further industrial
evelopments were to engulf the abbey
nvirons, including iron making and coal
nining. In spite of certain repairs by the
Neath Philosophical Society in 1848–49,
y the end of the nineteenth century
he whole complex had become a sorry
vergrown pile. One observer described
thus: 'Neglected Neath, once the
rnament of a lovely vale, looms up through
he dense veil of smoke, like the skeleton
f a stranded ship crumbling piecemeal
o decay under the influence of almost
erpetual rain'.

After years of further neglect, from 1924
group of local volunteers, led by Mr Glen
aylor, began to clear and partially excavate
he site. By the late 1930s, up to 4,000
ons of debris had been removed from
he church alone. In 1944 the abbey was
laced in the care of the State, and fresh
rogrammes of conservation and clearance
vere begun after the Second World War.
oday, Neath Abbey is maintained by Cadw,
he historic environment service of the
Welsh Assembly Government.

A reconstruction drawing showing the late sixteenth-century house, built over the south-east corner of the former abbey complex (Joanna Griffiths/RCAHMW).

This 1741 engraving of Neath Abbey by Samuel and Nathaniel Buck depicts the ruins of the abbey church in the right foreground. To the rear left is the Tudor and later house, shown with its roofs intact and chimneys smoking (National Library of Wales).

A Tour of the Abbey

An aerial view of Neath Abbey, looking west. At the heart of the monastic complex was the rectangular cloister, with the great cruciform church to the north (right) and the key monastic buildings, positioned alon the other three sides (RCAHMW).

Aside from its Savigniac origins, the layout of the abbey buildings at Neath eventually conformed in all essentials to the regular Cistercian plan. On the highest part of the site was a large church, set out on an east–west alignment. To the south were the principal ranges of monastic buildings, positioned around the three remaining sides of a large open court known as the cloister.

Somewhere to the east of this central complex there is likely to have been an infirmary for the sick and aged monks, and (for much of the abbey's history) there may have been a separate block of lodgings for the abbot in the same general area. To the west of the church and cloister there was almost certainly accommodation for guests of various standing. Other ancillary structures essential to the daily life and agricultural economy of the abbey lay within a much larger enclosed precinct, its bounds probably determined by a stone wall. The remains of one of the gatehouses, which regulated access to the monastery, survive to the north-west of the site.

This tour offers visitors one route around the abbey complex, but the site can be investigated in any order using the bird's-eye view (inside front cover) and the numbers noted in the text. To follow this tour, turn left from the site entrance and make your way over towards the cloister [**1**]. Walk along the gravel path on the left-hand side and continue through the doorway at the far end. Turn left, and find your way around to the west front of the abbey church [**2**].

The Church

Dedicated to St Mary, this great church was built between about 1280 and 1330, and was one of a group of new-style British Cistercian churches begun over the course of the thirteenth century. In broad terms, it was of a similar form to the church raised about 1241–55 at the comparatively recent white monk foundation of Netley in Hampshire. But it had even more in common with the church begun about 1269 by the community at Tintern Abbey in Monmouthshire. Just as at Tintern, Neath's new late thirteenth-century church replaced smaller and simpler Romanesque building, ne which had probably served the ommunity since before 1150.

The west front is a good position to onsider the scale and layout of the church s completed. A cruciform or cross-shaped uilding, it featured a long aisled nave at his end. In the middle distance, that is, at he central axis of the church, there was substantial 'crossing' with transepts to he north and south. At the far end was a ectangular eastern arm, or presbytery. The nain internal elevations were two storeys igh, and all the spaces were covered with tone rib vaults.

At the middle of the west front, flanked y very substantial buttresses, was a wide entral doorway, or portal. Above this, the pper part of the façade would have been lled with an enormous window, doubtless eaturing an ornate design of stone tracery o its head. Of the doorway itself, all that urvives today are the much-worn bases of s jambs. It is clear, however, that to either de of these jambs a pattern of 'blind' racery originally continued across the ower façade, fragments of which remain.

The space between the two buttresses vas enclosed with a stone-vaulted porch r narthex. This is often referred to as a alilee, since the abbot leading his monks procession into the church was thought o symbolize Christ leading his disciples nto Galilee.

Now go through the west doorway and egin to walk down the central part of the ave [**3**]. In Cistercian churches, this area was eserved for the lay brothers. Here at Neath, hey would have made their way into the uilding via the small doorway in the south-vest corner [**4**], having come from their uarters in the west range (p. 14). Along he full length of the nave you will see the ositions of two rows of clustered piers [**5**], vith each pair marking what is known as bay division. Hence, there were seven ays to the nave as a whole. The piers in urn supported pointed arches, the whole epresenting the lower half of the two-storey levation. The upper level, known as the lerestory, contained a row of windows with leep splays. Some indication of the form of he windows survives at the western end.

Above: The church at Neath Abbey was completely rebuilt between about 1280 and 1330. Its general form may be compared to the new church at Tintern Abbey, begun about 1269. In the west front, seen here, there would have been a great central doorway and a large traceried window above.

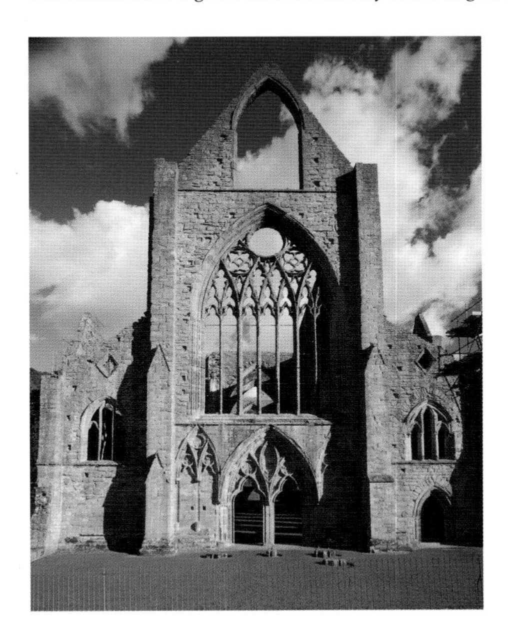

Above: The tracery of a large seven-light window survives in the west front at Tintern Abbey.

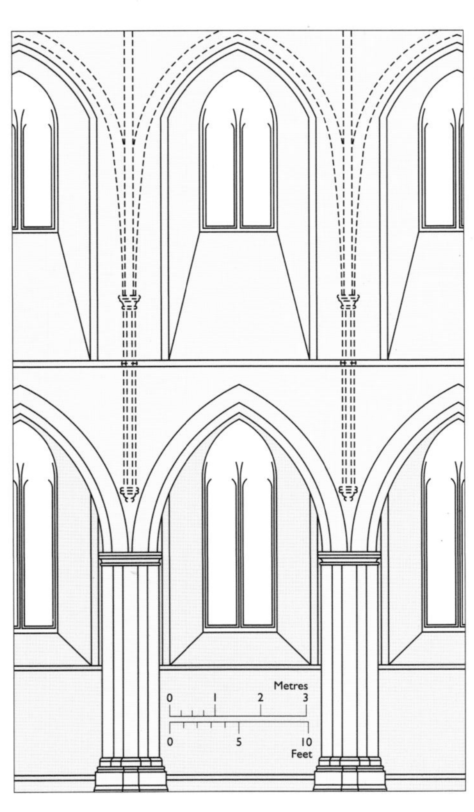

Right: A reconstruction drawing showing the likely form of the two-storey elevation in the nave at Neath (David Robinson/Chris Jones-Jenkins).

Above: A view looking north-west along the length of the nave towards the west front. In Cistercian churches the nave was initially reserved for the lay brothers. At the centre of the view is the position of the monks' choir.

Left: The figure of Christ in Majesty carved on one of the fourteenth-century stone bosses from the vaults in the abbey church.

A late thirteenth-century manuscript illustration of Cistercian monks at their devotions in the choir and presbytery (Stiftsbibliothek Zwettl, Ms 400, f. 1v).

The lay brothers' choir stalls were usually arranged with their backs to the piers, effectively closing off the nave aisles to the north and south. In the north aisle [**6**], notice the fragments of dressed stone surrounding the window jambs. There are subtle changes in the detailing from east to west, probably indicating different stages in the building programme. On the wall face below, set at regular intervals, are the remains of the triple-shaft groups that rose to support the vaults over the aisle. There are also extensive patches of medieval rendering covering the rubble masonry.

Across in the south aisle [**7**], the windows were smaller, and featured higher sills. This arrangement was intended to accommodate the cloister alley with its lean-to roof outside.

Further along the length of the church, the stone foundations [**8**] mark the position of the pulpitum. This was a solid screen wall which may have featured some form of decorative façade towards the nave. A central doorway in the pulpitum led into the monks' choir and presbytery [**9**]. Cut off by further screen walls on all sides, this area served almost as a distinct church set within the abbey church as a whole. The monks' wooden choir stalls sat on the stone foundations, which can be seen running eastwards from the back of the pulpitum [**10**]. Eight times each day, the brothers gathered here in their stalls to celebrate their services, or divine offices. Everything else in the daily routine of a Cistercian monk took second place to this constant round of prayer, the *opus Dei* or work of God as it was called.

Above the choir, and supported by four large central crossing piers, there was possibly a low tower or lantern. In which case, this must have housed the four bells from Neath which were eventually sold to a London merchant after the suppression of the house. At the far east end of the presbytery, the stone foundation marks the site of the high altar [**11**]. It was perhaps here, in this most sacred area of the church that the great stone vault overhead was at its finest. As we are told by the sixteenth-century poet, Lewis Morgannwg, the ceiling was 'painted with the arms of Kings and around them [were] the shields of princes'. He further wrote: 'Shining like the starry heaven is the vast and lofty roof, where there are painted the forms of archangels'.

The side aisles, or ambulatory, at the eastern end of the church served as a processional walk around the choir and presbytery [**12**]. Single window openings survive in the north and south aisles. Under the southern example are the remains of a doorway with decorative internal and external jambs. This is likely to have been the entrance into the church from the monks' infirmary.

There were four lesser altars against the east wall of the church, two at the centre and one in either aisle. Above the central pair would have been another huge traceried window in the gable of the building, perhaps featuring some of the stained glass referred to by Lewis Morgannwg: 'Manifold are the colours in the windows whereon figures are skilfully drawn through them beam forth rays of the sun'.

In the area around the eastern end of the church, you will find several large fragments of collapsed masonry in the greensward. To the north [**13**], one of these

ight: A collapsed fragment of masonry from the
orth aisle of the presbytery. At the centre is a
pringer', the point from which three vault ribs
rojected out across the aisle. The moulded arches
either side represent the adjacent aisle windows.*

*ar right: To one side of the altar in the
outhernmost chapel of the south transept there
e the remains of two rectangular recesses. In the
ft recess was a piscina, in which the water used
cleanse the sacred vessels was drained away. The
cess to the right was an aumbry or cupboard.*

agments retains a 'springer', the point from
hich three moulded vault ribs projected
ut over the presbytery aisle. To either side
f this are the arch mouldings of the two
djacent windows.

Throughout the abbey's history, this same
astern area [**14**] was almost certainly used
s the monks' cemetery. Indeed, traces of
everal graves were recently located in
xcavations outside the north-east corner
f the presbytery.

Next, retrace your steps back towards
e north transept [**15**]. Here, the most
rominent remains are those of the windows
the two eastern chapels. The chapel to
e left retains evidence of a step leading
p to the altar against the east wall. In the
ain body of the transept, a doorway in the
orthern wall probably gave access to the
onks' cemetery. Above this, the gable was
oubtless filled with another large window.

Over in the south transept [**16**], you
ill again find a pair of chapels on the east
ide, in this case with substantial remains
f the two altar bases. Notice, too, the
turgical features grouped in a rectangular
rchitectural frame in the outer wall of the
outhern chapel. In the broken recess to
he left there is clear evidence of a piscina
r sink. Here, a monk would cleanse the
acred vessels he had used in his private
Mass in the chapel. The squared recess
o the right was originally closed with a
vooden door, and probably served as
n aumbry or cupboard to store the
acred vessels. Further to the right of
hese features, there is a doorway that
ave access through to the sacristy.

Against the west wall of the transept, you
vill see the remains of the night stairs [**17**],
sed by the monks to enter the abbey
church from their dormitory during the
hours of darkness. On the line of these stairs,
there is a very fine stone handrail set into
the wall. Just above it — at the base of a
vault corbel — notice the attractive carved
stone face, a further indication of the quality
of workmanship employed in the building.

Leave the church by way of the
processional doorway in the south aisle
of the nave [**18**]. There are rich early
fourteenth-century mouldings to the
jambs on the outer face.

Above: During the hours of darkness, the monks entered the church from their dormitory by way of the night stairs in the south transept. Notice the fine stone handrail set into the adjacent wall.

Right: The liturgical importance of the processional doorway linking the cloister with the south aisle of the nave was signalled by its elaborate early fourteenth-century mouldings.

The Monastic Buildings

The cloister [1] was always at the heart of any medieval monastic complex. At Neath, the elongated north–south axis was due to the loss of the early abbey church, the position of which probably lay marginally to the south of its larger successor (see plan on inside back cover). The cloister was always an open space and may have served as a garden. It was surrounded on all four sides by passages known as cloister walks or alleys, probably with lean-to roofs, and with open rhythmic arcades facing on to the central garth. Some of the corbels, which supported the roof over the north walk, can be seen in the wall of the church.

The range of buildings along the eastern side of the cloister was reserved for the choir monks. A series of doorways opening from the adjacent cloister walk led into the ground-floor chambers. The first doorway, with its moulded jambs, gave access to the book room [**19**]. East of this was the sacristy [**20**], the room in which vestments and sacred vessels might be stored. There was a window in the east wall, and direct access to the church was provided via the doorway in the south transept.

Adjoining these was the chapter house [**21**], one of the most important rooms in the monastery. Its walls were very much reduced in the post-suppression history of the site, though it appears the stone-vaulted ceiling was once carried on four central piers, two of which survive. The monks gathered here each morning to hear a chapter of the *Rule of St Benedict* read by one of the brothers. This was also the room in which matters of secular business might be discussed, and where the monks confessed any faults and received punishment. It was not uncommon for the Cistercians to bury their abbots in the chapter house.

Next in the range came the parlour and the slype. The parlour [**22**] was the place where essential conversation could be conducted without breaking the cloister rule of silence. It may also have been used as an office for the prior, the man who served as the abbot's deputy. The slype, which survives rather better [**23**], was merely a passage through the range and gave access to the buildings east of the main cloister.

You should now walk through the slype and turn right, around to the eastern side of the building. The doorway, which sits below the small two-light window, leads to a pair of barrel-vaulted chambers (currently inaccessible). Further to the left (south), you will find another doorway leading into a large vaulted undercroft (a key is required for access). This superb five-bay rib-vaulted chamber is likely to have served as the monks' day room, and is a precious survival of Welsh Cistercian architecture. The vault ribs are carried on a row of four circular columns with moulded bases and capitals, and on moulded corbels set into the side walls. After the suppression, the chamber was retained virtually intact and may have been used as the servants' hall within the

The cloister seen from the south. It was always an open space, and was probably used as a garden. There were covered passageways or alleys on all four sides.

The handsome vaulted chamber at the southern end of the east range probably served as the monks' day room. It was retained in the post-suppression house when it could have been used as a servants' hall.

Left: This stone effigy of an ecclesiastic holding a model of a church has long been taken to represent Abbot Adam of Carmarthen (about 1266–89).

Above: The monks' first-floor dormitory was connected to their latrine building by a vaulted bridge, the piers of which survive. The bridge structure was adapted to become a porch in the Tudor house.

Right: The base of one of the intricate jambs that flanked the doorway to the monks' refectory.

udor great house (pp. 14–15). It now ouses an important collection of ourteenth-century floor tiles from the bbey, along with various fragments of ecorative stonework. The carved stone ffigy at the centre of the chamber is that f an ecclesiastic, with a model of a church eld in his left hand. There is a long-held elief that the figure represents Adam f Carmarthen, the abbot who probably egan the building of Neath's second abbey hurch in the late thirteenth century (p. 5).

On leaving the day room, stand on the mall terrace immediately outside. Behind ou, the entire upper floor of the east range vas occupied by the monks' dormitory [**24**], n which there may have been space for etween eighty and a hundred beds. Ahead f you, and running parallel with the east ange, are the remains of the monks' latrine uilding [**25**]. The two were linked by a ridge at first-floor level, carried on the square piers with angle-shafts that can still be seen in the intervening space. In the long narrow latrine building, the latrines themselves were situated above the main drain.

Make your way back through the slype and progress to the southern walk of the cloister. Immediately on the left, notice the remains of a flight of steps. These were the day stairs, the route by which the monks came down into the cloister during daylight hours. The room adjacent to these stairs was the warming house [**26**], the place where the monks were allowed to gather around a communal fire which was kept burning through the winter months.

The principal room in the south range was the monks' refectory [**27**]. The doorway is at the centre, marked by the bases of its jambs. Clearly, these would have been highly decorative features, with an intricate arrangement of attached and detached shafts. To either side of the doorway, there are traces of the shallow rectangular recesses that housed the lavers [**28**], large basins where the brothers washed their hands before going into meals. The bases of further decorative jambs mark the outer edges of the recesses. In the preferred Cistercian fashion, the refectory itself was arranged at right angles to the range. Its walls ran some way southwards of the cloister, though they appear to have been completely levelled when the Tudor mansion was constructed.

The last building in the south range was the kitchen [**29**]. Traces of the doorway from the cloister survive, as does the basic outline of the room. However, the monastic features were largely destroyed by the industrial workings of the eighteenth century and later. Furnaces and casting pits were found here when the site was first excavated.

The long two-storey range on the west side of the cloister was initially occupied almost exclusively by the lay brothers, or *conversi* (literally converts). The *conversi* were the backbone of the early Cistercian agricultural economy. They were mostly illiterate men, and were required by their specific rule book to remain so. Their accommodation was segregated from the cloister proper by a distinctly Cistercian feature known as a 'lane' [**30**]. This served as a passage linking the rooms on the ground floor of the range, and also gave access to the doorway in the south-west corner of the church [**4**].

Above: The range of buildings on the west side of the cloister was originally occupied by the abbey's lay brothers. Their refectory was probably on the ground floor at the southern end, seen here. The entire upper floor served as their dormitory.

Beginning at the southern end of the range [**31**], there were four rib-vaulted bays on the ground floor, which may well have served as the lay brothers' refectory. Next, the tunnel-vaulted passage at the middle of the range [**32**] was the main entrance to the cloister. A rib-vaulted porch was added to the outer side of this passage in the fourteenth century. North of this, there were three more stone-vaulted bays [**33**], some area of which is likely to have provided cellarage. The northernmost bay might have been screened off to form the outer parlour, with doors on the east and west sides. It was here that the cellarer — a senior monk with responsibility for the conduct of the *conversi* — might speak with up to two brothers at a time. The cellarer would also have had an office somewhere in the west range, possibly in one of the tunnel-vaulted bays at the north end. The entire upper floor of the range, lit by windows along both sides, served as the lay brothers' dormitory [**34**]. It was linked to their latrine at the south-west corner of the building [**35**].

From the mid-fourteenth century, as the number of lay brothers declined, the rooms in the west range must have been given over to other uses. After the suppression, the building was retained for some purpose. The chimneys, which can be seen high on the east wall at the southern end [**36**], again reflect eighteenth-century industrial activity.

A view of the west range from the north-west. The porch seems to have been added to an earlier passage through the range in the fourteenth century.

The Abbot's Lodging

Now make your way to the far southern side of the abbey site, and turn left to stand at the centre of the main façade of the late medieval abbot's lodging [**37**]. Dating from about 1500, the monastic work here can be difficult to distinguish from that of the later Tudor house (see below). Some clue, however, is provided by the pale yellow Bath Stone used in the windows and other dressings of the monastic phase.

At the centre of the new lodging was the southern end of the monks' dormitory [**24**] presumably converted to serve as a great hall. The abbot concerned also commandeered the former monks' latrine building to the east (right) [**25**]. The two blocks were in part connected by a projecting polygonal stair turret, introduced to improve access between floor levels [**38**]. To the west (left), the new building further projected across the southern end of the monks' refectory [**39**]. The abbot's withdrawing chambers were possibly located to this side. In all, the last few abbots of Neath would have occupied a highly comfortable suite of south-facing rooms, arranged over two and three storeys.

The Post-Suppression House

Following the closure of the abbey in 1539, it may have been Sir Richard Williams alias Cromwell who began to create a Tudor house over the former abbot's lodging (p. 6). Such conversions were very far from unusual in the wake of the suppression of the monasteries. Among the best-known examples in England, the country houses at Forde in Dorset and Woburn in Bedfordshire both incorporate a substantial amount of fabric from their medieval Cistercian predecessors. Similarly, Newstead Abbey in Nottinghamshire is raised over the monastic buildings of an Augustinian priory, and Lacock Abbey in Wiltshire reuses much of the former abbey of Augustinian canonesses.

In Wales, another very good example such a conversion is known from ›ath's neighbouring Cistercian abbey Margam. In this case it was Sir Rice ›nsel (d. 1559) of Oxwich who created ubstantial residence to the south-east the abbey church. Described in the 90s as a 'faire and sumptious house', › building was expanded in the Classical le during the seventeenth century. ›wever it was gradually abandoned er the 1770s.

At Neath, although parts of the house ›re perhaps completed by about 1560, ›er features suggest ongoing work closer the end of the sixteenth century. In the finished house was of formidable ›le, comprising two main storeys with ics. Much of the accommodation on › ground floor consisted of the barely ›ered monastic spaces, with the main ›roach leading to the north front. The ›mer bridge structure linking the monks' rmitory and latrine was used as a porch, ›essed between the unequal halves the façade. The monks' day room was ›ained very much intact and may have ›en used as a servants' hall.

All of the principal rooms were on › first floor. They are easily distinguished their generally large mullioned and ›nsomed rectangular windows executed reused creamy white Sutton Stone — st viewed from the west. The large upper ›ening, which has lost its window tracery 0], marks the position of a grand bay ›ndow. It lit one end of what must have ›en a very impressive long gallery spanning › house from east to west [**41**]. It was ›obably this gallery which led to a remark ›ade in 1684 that 'the house is famous › one of the fairest Rooms in Wales'. The ›er main rooms led off the long gallery, ›th a great chamber to the south [**42**]. The e brand new wing in the house was at › north-east corner [**43**]. On the ground or, you will find the remains of the kitchen ›th its two large fireplaces [**44**].

Interestingly, the abbey church was not ›elled completely by the Williams family their successors, but must have been ›tained as some form of Gothic folly, ›obably within an attractive garden setting.

Above: About 1500, one of the last abbots of Neath created a new set of lodgings by converting various buildings at the south side of the site. These lodgings were used as the basis for a much larger house begun by the Williams (alias Cromwell) family after the suppression of the abbey.

Above: Margam House, shown here in an anonymous painting of about 1700, was created from the buildings of the Cistercian abbey at nearby Margam by Sir Rice Mansel (d. 1559) of Oxwich (Private Collection).

The Abbey Gatehouse

A short walk under the railway bridge to the north, and then westward along the A4230, brings you to the site of the abbey's inner or great gatehouse [**45**]. The remains are those of the rooms on the northern side of the gate-passage, which itself stood where the pavement and road now lie.

Traffic would have approached from the west (left). The room on this side (behind the low doorway) may have been a porter's lodge. To the right (east) are two large open arches that flanked the passage. Between the two sections, a surviving jamb marks the position of the gates by which the porter controlled the flow of both wheeled and pedestrian traffic through into the monastery.

The surviving fragment of the abbey's inner, or great, gatehouse. The remains are those of the rooms on the northern side of the gate-passage.

The Neath Tile Collection

A particularly remarkable feature of the ruins at Neath is the preservation into modern times of a vast quantity of superb medieval ceramic floor tiles. Most of these come from the abbey church, though some have been found in the cloister walks and surrounding buildings.

The construction of the new abbey church was completed in the early fourteenth century. As one of the final works, elaborately patterned tile pavements were laid on the floors of the monks' choir and presbytery, the ambulatory aisles, and the transepts and their chapels. The designs varied from one area to another, but each included a strong heraldic theme, with up to thirty different shields of arms represented on individual tiles. Other tiles carried hunting scenes, and many featured window tracery designs. The unity of the scheme as a whole is emphasized by the fact that the tiles were all made from the same fabric. They are thought to have been laid about 1340.

Antiquarian collectors began digging for specimens of these splendid tiles in the early nineteenth century, but fortunately large areas of the pavements remained intact. For conservation reasons, however, these had to be lifted in the late 1980s. The collection is now displayed in the stone-vaulted chamber that served as the monks' day room.

Above: These two fourteenth-century tiles from the church at Neath Abbey depict the legendary combat between King Richard I (left) and Saladin (right) (National Museum of Wales).

Above: The very substantial collection of floor tiles from Neath features a wide variety of individual designs. For example, the tile shown here to the left bears one of thirty different depictions of shields of arms known from the site; the architectural pattern to the right is based on near-contemporary forms of window tracery (National Museum of Wales).

Further Reading

Walter de Gray Birch, *A History of Neath Abbey* (Neath 1902).

Janet Burton, *Monastic and Religious Orders in Britain, 1000–1300* (Cambridge 1994).

L. A. S. Butler, *Neath Abbey* (HMSO, London 1976).

Lawrence Butler, 'Neath Abbey: The Twelfth-Century Church', *Archaeologia Cambrensis* **133** (1984), 147–51.

F. G. Cowley, *The Monastic Order in South Wales, 1066–1349* (Cardiff 1977).

Bennett D. Hill, *English Cistercian Monasteries and their Patrons in the Twelfth Century* (Urbana 1968), 80–115.

Christopher Holdsworth, 'The Affiliation of Savigny', in M. L. Dutton, D. M. La Corte and P. Lockey (editors), *Truth as Gift: Studies in Honor of John R. Sommerfeldt*, Cistercian Studies Series, **204** (Kalamazoo 2004), 43–88.

Laurence Ince, *Neath Abbey and the Industrial Revolution* (Stroud 2001).

David Robinson (editor), *The Cistercian Abbeys of Britain: Far from the Concourse of Men* (London 1998); reprinted in paperback (London 2002).

David M. Robinson, *The Cistercians in Wales: Architecture and Archaeology 1130–1540* (London 2006).

The Royal Commission on Ancient and Historical Monuments in Wales, 'Neath Abbey', in *An Inventory of the Ancient Monuments in Glamorgan, IV, i: The Greater Houses* (Cardiff 1981), 78–89.

Mary Suydam, 'Origins of the Savignac Order: Savigny's Role within Twelfth-Century Monastic Reform', *Revue Bénédictine* **86** (1976), 94–108.

David H. Williams, *The Welsh Cistercians*, new edition (Leominster 2001).

Glanmor Williams, 'Neath Abbey', in Elis Jenkins (editor), *Neath and District: A Symposium*, 2nd edition (Neath 1974), 73–91.